A Guide for Using

The Great Kapok Tree

in the Classroom

Based on the book written by Lynne Cherry

This guide written by **Lynn DiDominicis**

Teacher Created Resources, Inc.
12621 Western Avenue
Garden Grove, CA 92841
www.teachercreated.com
ISBN: 978-1-57690-084-0
©1997 Teacher Created Resources, Inc.
Reprinted, 2016
Made in U.S.A.

Illustrated by
Barb Lorseyedi

Edited by
Stephanie Buehler, M.P.W., M.A.

Cover Art by
Wendy Chang

Table of Contents

Introduction and Sample Lessons

A good book can touch the lives of children like a good friend. Pictures, words, and characters can inspire young minds as they turn to literary treasures for companionship, adventure, and guidance. Great care has been taken in selecting the books and activities in the Literature Unit series in order to challenge students, build their skills, and create interest. Teachers can use all of the unit activities or choose those that best supplement their own valuable ideas.

A Sample Lesson Plan

The sample lessons below provide the teacher with a specific sequence of lesson plan suggestions. Each of the lessons can take from one to several days to complete and can include all or some of the suggested activities. Refer to the "Suggestions for Using the Unit Activities" on pages 6–9 for information related to the unit activities.

A Unit Planner

For the teacher who wishes to tailor the suggestions on pages 6–9 into a format other than the one provided here, use the blank unit planner on page 4. Reproduce copies of the Unit Planner as needed.

Sample Lesson Plan

Lesson 1
- Introduce the book by using all or some of the activities on page 6.
- Read "About the Author" on page 5.
- Read *The Great Kapok Tree* aloud.

Lesson 2
- Read *The Great Kapok Tree* a second time.
- Prepare the pocket charts and use the "Story Questions" and activities to involve students in critical thinking (pages 10–13).
- Have students complete "Pocket Chart Activities" (pages 10–12).
- Use the pocket chart "Story Summary Sentence Strips" (pages 14–17).

Lesson 3
- Complete activities 5 and 6 on page 8.
- Make a story map (page 21).
- Reproduce "Brain Teaser" and have the class complete it (page 22).
- Begin preparing puppets for the story dramatization (pages 23–26).

Lesson 4
- Prepare and present the dramatization.
- Play the board game "Follow the Snake" (page 27).
- Write "Rain Forest Poem" (page 28).
- Practice subtraction skills by using activities 12 and 13 on page 9.
- Create the "Door Knob Hanging Tree" (page 31).
- Begin research project (pages 33–36).

Lesson 5
- Have the class write a "Rain Forest Rap" (page 32).
- Continue the research project.

Lesson 6
- Have students send messages to their state representatives (page 37).
- Complete and display the research project.

Lesson 7
- Culminating Activity: Create a rain forest environment in the classroom using the instructions on pages 38–46.

Unit Planner

Unit Activities	Unit Activities
Date:	Date:
Notes/Comments:	Notes/Comments:

Unit Activities	Unit Activities
Date:	Date:
Notes/Comments:	Notes/Comments:

Unit Activities	Unit Activities
Date:	Date:
Notes/Comments:	Notes/Comments:

Getting to Know the Book and Author

(*The Great Kapok Tree* © 1990 by Lynne Cherry, published by Harcourt Brace & Company)

About the Book

Two men enter the Amazon rain forest in Brazil. One man is told to chop down a kapok tree. He begins to chop with his ax, but it is hard work. Soon he falls asleep beneath the great tree.

As he sleeps, the creatures of the rain forest who depend upon the kapok tree for their existence begin to whisper in the man's ear. They plead with him not to chop down their tree, telling him, "All living things depend on one another" and "What happens tomorrow depends upon what you do today." A rain forest child asks the man to look with new eyes upon the great tree.

The man awakens, picks up his ax and then hesitates. Dropping the ax at the base of the tree, he walks out of the rain forest.

About the Author

Lynne Cherry was born on January 5, 1952, in Philadelphia, Pennsylvania, where she grew up and attended the Tyler School of Art. After graduating from college, she worked as an illustrator, creating artwork for many books written by other authors, including several *Ranger Rick* books published by the National Wildlife Federation.

Lynne Cherry considers herself an activist, a person who works hard to make the world a better place, especially the rain forest. Cherry became concerned about this special environment when she traveled to the Amazon rain forest in Brazil and was taken by its beauty and the marvelous creatures that inhabited it. She wanted to help save this treasure, so she wrote and illustrated *The Great Kapok Tree*. She began making her illustrations as she sat in the rain forest, monkeys swinging in the trees overhead and animals scurrying by her feet. This book has had tremendous response from its readers, both in terms of enjoying the book and in working to save the rain forest. The book has received many notices of recognition. It became a Reading Rainbow Review Book and an American Bookseller's "Pick of the Lists."

Lynne Cherry lives in both Connecticut in a farmhouse that she turned into an artist's house and in Princeton, New Jersey. She continues her life's mission through her artwork, which she states is "a wonderful way to express the beauty I see in life."

Suggestions for Using the Unit Activities

Use some or all of the following suggestions to introduce students to *The Great Kapok Tree* and to extend their appreciation of the book through activities across the curriculum. The suggested activities have been divided into three sections to assist the teacher in planning the literature unit.

- **Before the Book** includes suggestions for preparing the classroom environment prior to reading the literature.

- **Into the Book** has activities that focus on the book's content, characters, theme, etc.

- **After the Book** extends the reader's enjoyment of the book with a culminating activity.

Before the Book

1. Before you begin the unit, prepare the vocabulary cards, story questions, and sentence strips for the pocket chart activities (see samples, patterns, and directions on pages 10–17).

2. Prepare a book corner with books and materials about the rain forest. The bibliography on pages 47 and 48 can be used as a resource.

3. If you teach thematically, this book will work well with *Our Environment, Rain Forest* (Intermediate Extended Thematic Unit), *Plants* (Primary), *Endangered Species* (Primary), and *Ecology* (Primary), all available from Teacher Created Resources.

4. Introduce the story by connecting it to previous experiences or knowledge. Ask the following questions as a springboard to discussion:

   - Have you been to the zoo? Which animals do you remember?

   - Do you know which of these animals might be found in a rain forest?

   - What kind of vegetation would you find in the rain forest? How do you know that?

5. Reproduce copies of "Rain Forest Vocabulary" on page 18. Have the students work alone or in pairs to complete the activities. Then have a class discussion about the vocabulary meanings, using a dictionary or context clues for assistance.

6. Look at the outside and inside covers of *The Great Kapok Tree*. Identify areas of the world where the rain forest is found and note the different animals.

The Great Kapok Tree   *Language Arts*

Name _____

Rain Forest Vocabulary

Look at each word below. Think about how the word was used in the story. Remember to use the words around a new word to help you understand its meaning. Write what you think the meaning is for each of these words.

1. creatures _____
   _____

2. ancestors _____

3. generations _____
   _____

4. hive _____
   _____

5. pollinate _____

6. troupe _____

7. understory _____
   _____

8. oxygen _____
   _____

9. fragrant _____
   _____

Suggestions for Using the Unit Activities *(cont.)*

Into the Book

1. **Story Questions:** Develop critical thinking skills using the story questions on page 13. The questions are based on Bloom's Taxonomy and are provided for each of Bloom's levels of learning. Following directions on page 11, reproduce copies of the monkey on page 12. Write story questions on the monkeys and then use the accompanying activities. Directions on how to make a pocket chart are on page 10.

2. **Vocabulary:** Discuss the meanings of the vocabulary words below by using them in context. Then direct the students to the pocket chart vocabulary activity on page 10.

creatures	sweat	lulled
gash	ancestors	generations
hive	pollen	pollinate
depend	troupe	canopy
understory	oxygen	fragrant

3. **Vocabulary Game:** The vocabulary game on page 11 is an opportunity to put new words into actual use. Students may work in cooperative groups to complete this activity.

4. **Sentence Strips:** Cut apart and laminate the sentences on pages 14–17 to use with a pocket chart. (See page 11 for details.) Complete some or all of the following activities:

   • On the pocket chart, sequence the sentences in the order in which the events happened in the story.

   • Use the sentences to retell the story.

   • Divide the class into small groups and distribute a few sentence strips to each group, asking them to act out the part of the story to which the sentences refer.

   In addition to these activities, you may wish to reproduce the pages and have each student read the sentences aloud to a partner or take them home to read to a parent, sibling, or friend.

Suggestions for Using the Unit
Activities *(cont.)*

Into the Book *(cont.)*

5. **Using Verbs:** Reproduce the "Rain Forest Frolics" activity on page 19. Working alone, in pairs, or in cooperative groups, have your students find the "action" words in the story. Have each group (or student) choose some words to act out and let the rest of the class guess the word. Write a new story using as many of these words as possible.

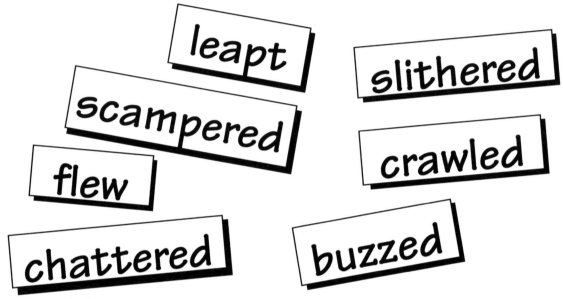

6. **Reading Consonant Blends:** Review the concept of consonant blends with students and then brainstorm a few examples. Reproduce the "Boa Constrictor's Consonant Blends" activity on page 20. Complete the activity and use it as a springboard for these decoding skills. Group the words on a chart, finding similar patterns of consonant blends. Finally, find the words in the story and discuss.

7. **Story Map:** Have students work in groups to make story maps on butcher paper. (A story map diagram is provided on page 21.) Make copies of the direction card on page 21 and give each group a card. When groups complete their story maps, incorporate them as part of the rain forest environment culminating activity.

8. **Brain Teaser:** Reproduce the activity on page 22 and have the class complete it.

9. **Dramatization:** Have students retell the story using marionettes. Directions for construction of a stage and marionettes are on page 23. Patterns can be found on pages 24–26. *The Great Kapok Tree* features strong usage of verbs. Using verbs as a basis for storytelling is a good way to create active play. One way to begin is to match each animal in the story with the verb the author uses. Then write sentences using the animal and its verb. Use these sentences as part of the puppet script.

10. **Board Game:** Reproduce page 27. Have students color the patterns and the game board. Laminate them for durability. Make small circle game pieces and use a die. When a player lands on the tail of a snake, he or she follows its body to the space where the head is located. Students move up the game board. The first player to reach the end is the winner.

Suggestions for Using the Unit Activities *(cont.)*

Into the Book *(cont.)*

11. **Rain Forest Poem:** Reproduce page 28. Have the class brainstorm some rain forest words that rhyme. Then write two lines of the poem as a class. Have each student finish the poem individually. Design a cover and make a class book.

12. **Subtraction:** Ask the class what they notice about the number 11. (It is an odd number, made using two numeral ones, one more than 10, add elevens sequentially and get a sequence of 11–22–33, etc.)

    • Make 11 manipulatives from the monkey pattern on page 24.

    • Perform subtraction problems with the class, using the monkeys as manipulatives.

    • Demonstrate and make up number sentences.

    • Make up some story problems.

    • Reproduce the activity on page 29 and use it as a timed activity.

13. **Rain Forest Subtraction:** Reproduce the activity on page 30 and use it for reinforcement.

14. **Art:** Reproduce the door hanger pattern on page 31 onto tagboard. Have a class discussion about how to conserve energy in our homes. Ask the students to take the tree home and hang it on a door knob as a reminder.

15. **Music:** Follow the instructions on page 32 and create a rain forest rap as an oral activity. See the bibliography for further information on ordering a rap from the World Wildlife Fund. Add a simple tune or rhythm instrument to your rap for interest.

16. **Research Project:** Using the ideas and instructions on pages 33–36, complete a research project with your class. You can use any traditional or multimedia encyclopedia and/or reference books. A list of resources can be found in the bibliography. The software program by Sunburst, *A Field Trip to the Rain Forest*, is excellent.

17. **Send a Message:** Reproduce the note card on page 37 and have students write a note to send to their congressperson.

After the Book

Culminating Activity: Create a Rain Forest Environment

Create a rain forest environment in your classroom. The step-by-step instructions are provided on pages 38–46.

Pocket Chart Activities

Prepare a pocket chart for storing and using toucan vocabulary cards, the monkey story questions (see patterns, page 12), and the sentence strips (pages 14–17).

How to Make a Pocket Chart

If a commercial chart is unavailable, you can make a pocket chart with access to a laminator. Begin by laminating a 24" x 36" (60 cm x 90 cm) piece of colored tagboard. Run about 20" (50 cm) of additional plastic. To make nine pockets, cut the clear plastic into nine equal strips. Space the strips equally down the 36" (90 cm) length of the tagboard. Attach each strip with cellophane tape along the bottom and sides. This chart will hold sentence strips, word cards, etc., and can be displayed in a learning center or mounted on a chalk tray for use with a group. A sample chart is provided below.

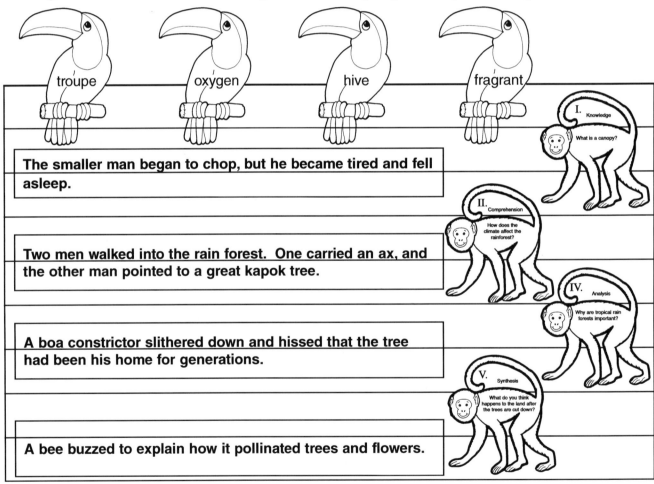

How to Use the Pocket Chart

1. Make vocabulary cards by reproducing the toucan pattern (page 12) on red or green construction paper or tagboard. Write vocabulary words on the toucans. (See the vocabulary list on page 7.) Use the toucan-shaped vocabulary cards to familiarize the children with the meanings of the difficult words or by giving them context clues. Place these cards along the top of your pocket chart.

Pocket Chart Activities *(cont.)*

2. Play a vocabulary game in cooperative groups. Divide the blackboard or a large piece of butcher paper into columns corresponding to your reading groups. At a signal, have each group send a runner to the pocket chart to pick a word (see words listed on page 7). The runner returns to his or her group, and together the group creates a sentence using the word. Next, a writer from the same group returns to the board or paper to write down the sentence with the vocabulary word left blank, e.g., "There are many_____ in the rain forest." Students from other teams earn points by guessing the missing vocabulary word. Words can be chosen until all have been used. The vocabulary word cards are then distributed at random to each group. (Be sure to keep each group's cards in a separate pile to ensure that they do not get their own cards.) The group receiving the vocabulary card is responsible for writing the word in the correct sentence. When everyone is finished, the whole class decides if the words have been placed correctly.

3. The sentence strips can be used to practice oral reading or to sequence story events. Reproduce pages 14–17 and laminate them for durability. Cut out the sentence strips or prepare sentences of your own to use with the pocket chart. These sentences are adapted from *The Great Kapok Tree*© and appear with the permission of Harcourt Brace & Company.

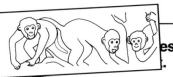

A troupe of monkeys scampered down and chattered about the rain forest becoming a desert.

A jaguar growled that the birds and animals he ate lived in the tree.

4. Reproduce copies of the monkey (page 12), using several sheets for each of six different colors. Use one color of paper to represent each of Bloom's levels of learning.

Example:

    I. Knowledge (*light brown*)

   II. Comprehension (*green*)

 III. Application (*yellow*)

 IV. Analysis (*orange*)

  V. Synthesis (*red*)

 VI. Evaluation (*lavender*)

Write a question from page 13 on the appropriate color-coded monkey. Write the level of the question on the top line. Laminate the monkeys for durability.

The following activities can be used to help the children develop and practice higher level critical thinking skills by using the questions on the color-coded monkeys:

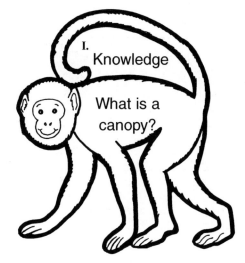

- Use a specific color-coded set of cards to question students at a particular level of learning.

- Give a set of cards, some from each level, to a cooperative group or pair and have them answer the questions.

Pocket Chart Patterns

See pages 10 and 11 for directions.

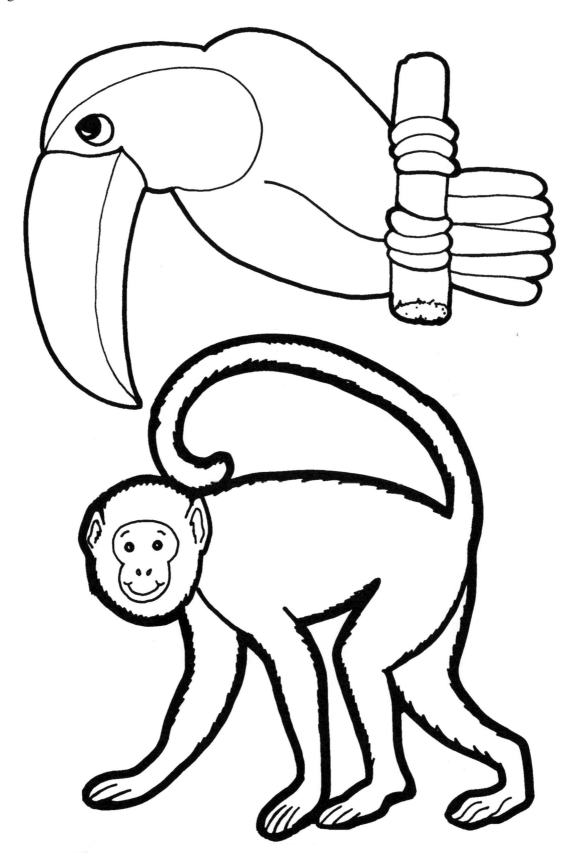

Story Questions

The following questions are based on Bloom's levels of learning.

Prepare the monkeys as directed on page 11. Write a different question from the levels of learning on each of the monkeys. Use the monkeys with the suggested activities in the unit.

I. Knowledge (ability to recall learned information)

- Name some of the animals that appear in the rain forest.

- What is a canopy?

- Name the birds that spoke in the man's ear. What did they say?

- What did the man do when he woke up?

II. Comprehension (basic understanding of information)

- Why was the kapok tree so important to the animals?

- What does the phrase "All living things depend on one another" mean?

- How does the climate affect the rain forest?

III. Application (ability to do something new with the information)

- How can we use products from the rain forest without destroying our environment?

- What can we do to help save the rain forests?

IV. Analysis (ability to examine the parts of a whole)

- Why do you think the men wanted to cut down the trees?

- Why are tropical rain forests important?

V. Synthesis (ability to bring together information to make something new)

- What do you think happens to the land after the trees are cut down?

- Can you think of anything else in the earth's environment that needs to be conserved?

VI. Evaluation (ability to form and defend an opinion)

- Do you think the rain forest should be saved? Why or why not?

- Would you recommend this story to a friend? Why or why not?

Sentence Strips

See pages 7 and 11 for directions on how to prepare and use these sentence strips.

Two men went to the rain forest. One carried an ax, and the other man pointed to a great kapok tree.

The smaller man began to chop, but he became tired and fell asleep.

A boa constrictor slithered down and hissed that the tree had been his home for generations.

A bee buzzed to explain how it pollinated trees and flowers.

Sentence Strips *(cont.)*

See pages 7 and 11 for directions on how to prepare and use these sentence strips.

A troupe of monkeys scampered down and chattered about the rain forest becoming a desert.

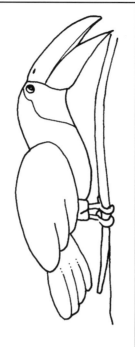

A toucan squawked that setting fires ruined the beauty of the rain forest.

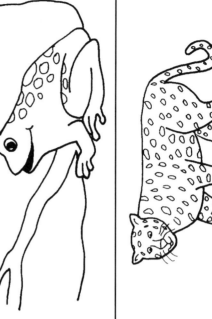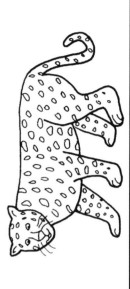

A small tree frog squeaked that chopping down the great kapok tree would leave him homeless.

A jaguar growled that the birds and animals he ate lived in the tree.

Sentence Strips *(cont.)*

See pages 7 and 11 for directions on how to prepare and use these sentence strips.

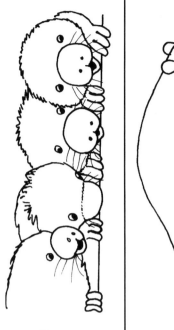

Four tree porcupines whispered that the trees produced oxygen.

The anteater said if you chop down the trees today, there will be no trees tomorrow.

A three-toed sloth plodded over and slowly spoke about how beautiful the rain forest is.

A child from the Yanomamo tribe asked the man to look at the world around him again.

Sentence Strips *(cont.)*

See pages 7 and 11 for directions on how to prepare and use these sentence strips.

The man awoke to see the creatures staring at him.

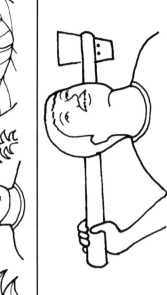

The man looked around him at the beauty of the rain forest.

The man got up, found his ax, and then looked around him again.

The man decided not to chop down the tree and left the rain forest.

Name _____

Rain Forest Vocabulary

Look at each word below. Think about how the word was used in the story. Remember to use the words around a new word to help you understand its meaning. Write what you think the meaning is for each of these words.

1. creatures _____

_____

2. ancestors _____

_____

3. generations _____

_____

4. hive _____

_____

5. pollinate _____

_____

6. troupe _____

_____

7. understory _____

_____

8. oxygen _____

_____

9. fragrant _____

_____

Rain Forest Frolics

Can you find 25 **ACTION** words?

_____

_____ _____ _____

_____ _____ _____

_____ _____ _____

_____ _____ _____

_____ _____ _____

_____ _____ _____

_____ _____ _____

_____ _____ _____

Boa Constrictor's Consonant Blends

> When **two** consonants follow one another within a word to form a blended sound, it is called a consonant blend.

1. Underline the consonant blends.
2. Say the words aloud.

- creatures
- sweat
- troupe
- fragrant
- scampered
- squawked
- clinging
- squawking
- slowly
- frog

- slithered
- smoldering
- crawled
- growled
- swung
- plodding
- small
- bright
- squeaky
- sloth

Example: **gr**oup, **tr**oupe

A **gr**oup of toucans and rattlesnakes formed a **tr**oupe.

3. Write some new words with consonant blends.

_____   _____   _____

_____   _____   _____

_____   _____   _____

_____   _____   _____

_____   _____   _____

_____   _____   _____

_____   _____   _____

4. Say the new words aloud.

Story Map

Sample Diagram

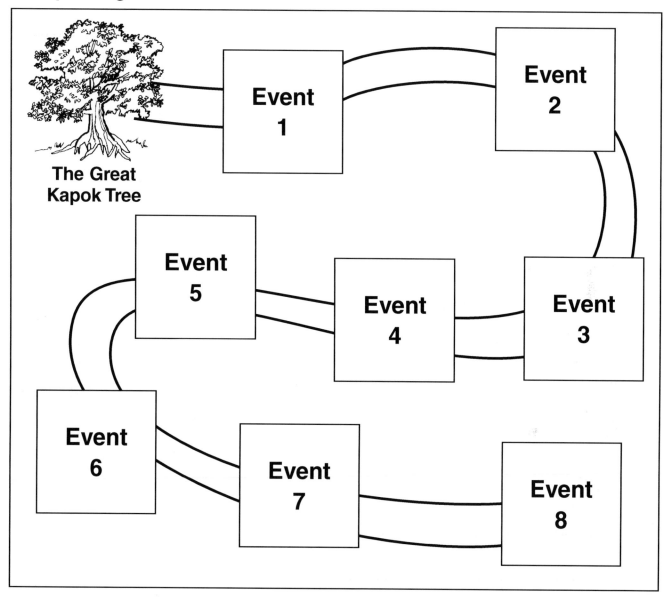

Note: Students can add rain forest illustrations to their story maps.

Directions:

1. Think of the important events in the story. Use your sentence strips to help you.

2. Draw a picture of each of the important events and color them.

3. Write a sentence to go with each picture.

4. Cut out the pictures and sentences.

5. Glue them on a large sheet of paper.

6. Draw arrows to make a path from one picture to the next.

7. Display your story map.

Brain Teaser

Four children—Mandi, Chantel, Brendan, and David—recently visited the Brookfield Zoo to see their favorite rain forest animals. One child liked monkeys, another liked toucans, a third liked boa constrictors, and a fourth liked jaguars. While at the zoo, each child ate one of the following: a corn dog, a hot dog, a slice of pizza, popcorn. Using the clues below, determine each child's favorite animal and what he or she had to eat. Mark an X in each correct box.

1. The girls liked the toucans and jaguars, while the boys liked the monkeys and boa constrictors.
2. Brendan ate his food on a stick, while Mandi ate pepperoni.
3. Chantel's favorite animal is a bird.
4. The boy who loves the monkeys also loves hot dogs.

	monkey	toucan	boa constrictor	jaguar	corn dog	hot dog	pizza	popcorn
Mandi								
Chantel								
Brendan								
David								

Note to teacher: Fold these answers under before reproducing.

Mandi—jaguar and pizza

Chantel—toucan and popcorn

Brendan—boa constrictor and corn dog

David—monkey and hot dog

The Great Kapok Tree: A Dramatization

Puppet Stage

Materials:

- a large box with two sides removed to create a stage
- construction paper
- string
- bath and paper towel tubes
- real plant life

Directions:

Create a rain forest environment inside the box with a kapok tree in the middle. Add birds, butterflies, and flowers.

Marionettes

Make marionettes by cutting out patterns provided on pages 24–26, coloring them, and laminating or gluing them onto tagboard. Use string to attach them to craft sticks.

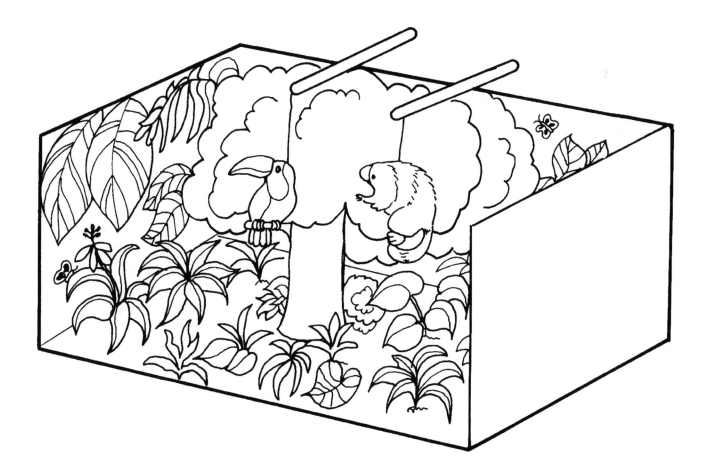

The Great Kapok Tree:
A Dramatization *(cont.)*

Patterns for Marionettes

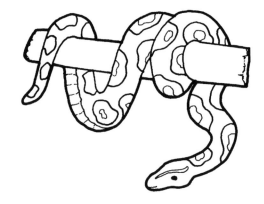

Boa Constrictor

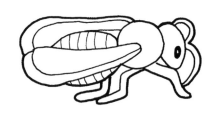

Bee

Monkey

Toucan

Macaw

Cock-of-the-Rock

The Great Kapok Tree: A Dramatization *(cont.)*

Patterns for Marionettes *(cont.)*

Anteater

Tree Frog

Jaguar

Tree Porcupine

The Great Kapok Tree: A Dramatization *(cont.)*

Patterns for Marionettes *(cont.)*

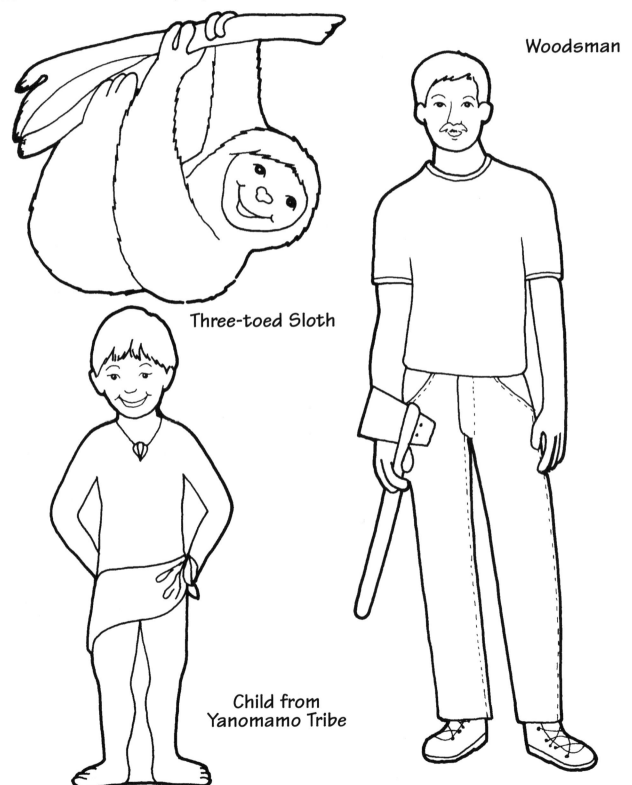

Woodsman

Three-toed Sloth

Child from
Yanomamo Tribe

Follow the Snake Game Board

70	69	50	49	30	29	10	9
71	68	51	48	31	28	11	8
72	67	52	47	32	27	12	7
73	66	53	46	33	26	13	6
74	65	54	45	34	25	14	5
75	64	55	44	35	24	15	4
76	63	56	43	36	23	16	3
77	62	57	42	37	22	17	2
78	61	58	41	38	21	18	1
END	60	59	40	39	20	19	GO

Rain Forest Poem

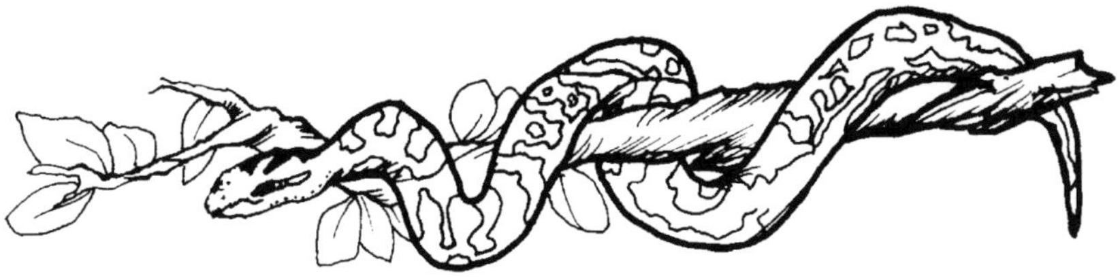

_____

_____

_____

_____

_____

_____

_____

_____

_____

_____

_____

This poem was written

by _____

Name _____

Through the Rain Forest

Solve each subtraction problem along the rain forest path. How fast can you get to the end?

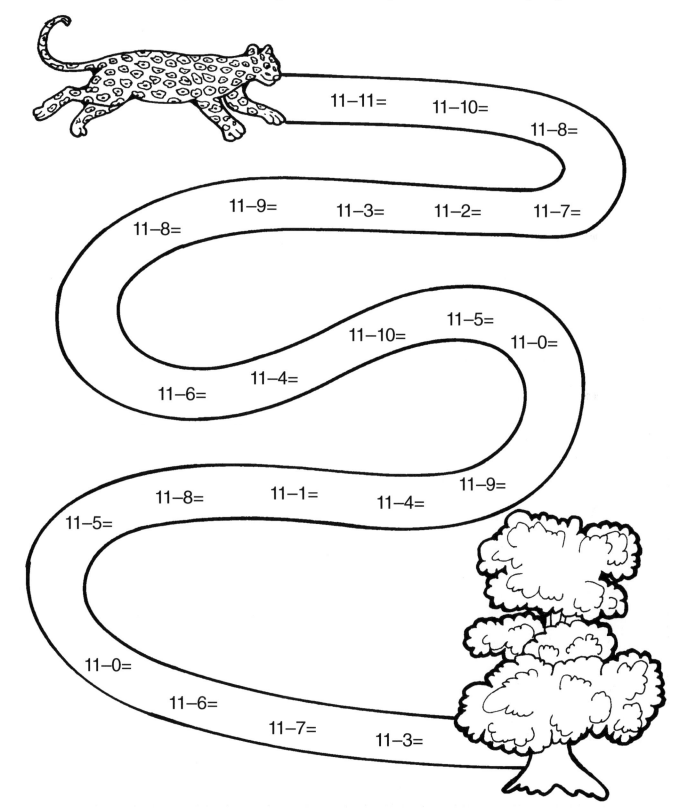

11–11=   11–10=

11–8=

11–9=   11–3=   11–2=   11–7=

11–8=

11–5=

11–0=

11–10=

11–4=

11–6=

11–9=

11–8=   11–1=   11–4=

11–5=

11–0=

11–6=

11–7=   11–3=

Name _____

Rain Forest Subtraction

Read the problems and then write a subtraction sentence for each one.

1. There were 21 monkeys in a tree. Nine of them went home. How many monkeys were left?

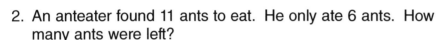

2. An anteater found 11 ants to eat. He only ate 6 ants. How many ants were left?

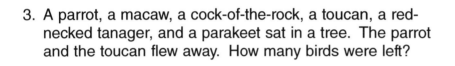

3. A parrot, a macaw, a cock-of-the-rock, a toucan, a red-necked tanager, and a parakeet sat in a tree. The parrot and the toucan flew away. How many birds were left?

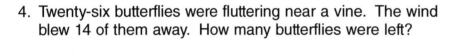

4. Twenty-six butterflies were fluttering near a vine. The wind blew 14 of them away. How many butterflies were left?

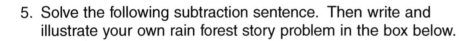

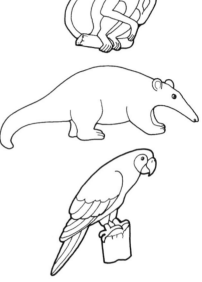

5. Solve the following subtraction sentence. Then write and illustrate your own rain forest story problem in the box below.

    15–8=_____

_____

_____

_____

_____

_____

_____

_____

_____

Door Knob Hanging Tree

Cut out the pattern and color your door knob hanging tree.

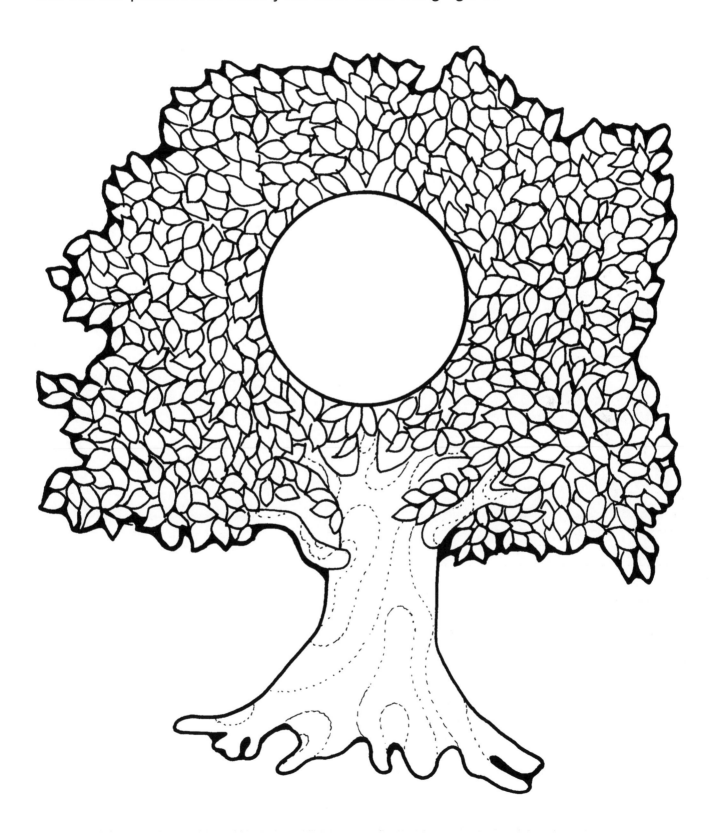

Rain Forest Rap

A rap is created by combining a repeatable phrase with information that is spoken in rhythm and, usually, rhyme. Create your own rain forest rap by using the suggestions below.

Brainstorm some descriptive phrases about the rain forest.

_____

_____

_____

_____

Write factual information in rhythmic, rhyming sentences.

_____

_____

_____

_____

_____

_____

_____

_____

_____

_____

_____

_____

To rap:

• Say your descriptive phrase.

• Chant the information sentence.

• Repeat your descriptive phrase after each information sentence or sentence grouping.

• Use percussion sounds to add interest to your rap.

Rain Forest Research Project

My
Rain Forest
Research
Project

Name _____

Rain Forest Research Project *(cont.)*

Activities

1. Make a list of the animals found in the rain forest.

2. Make a list of the plants found in the rain forest.

3. Create an animal data fact sheet. Include the name, class, weight, length, classification, and time when the animal is active (day or night). An example has been done for you.

Name	Class	Weight	Length	Classifi-cation	Day or Night
Anteater	Mammal	12 pounds	36"	Carnivore	Both

4. Create a plant data fact sheet. Include the name, type, if it produces fruit or seeds, and how it is pollinated. An example has been done for you.

Name	Type	Fruit or Seed	Pollinator
Brazil nut	tree	nut	bees

5. Make a food chain. Begin by drawing one animal and then adding the animal which it eats. Continue drawing animals, one after the other, until the chain is complete.

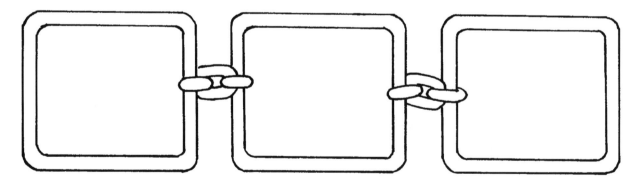

6. Find the answers to these questions:

   • Why do more kinds of animals live in the rain forest than any other part of the world?

   • How do rain forest animals find their food?

   • How do rain forest animals protect themselves?

   • What are some products that come from the rain forest?

7. *(Optional)* Take a field trip to the zoo. Record the animals you see and any information you find about them. Make a comparison between animals from Africa and animals from the rain forest.

Rain Forest Research Project *(cont.)*

Rain Forest Animal Data Sheet

Name of the animal: _____

Draw a picture of the animal.

Interesting Information

Its unique characteristics:

_____

_____

_____

What it eats:

_____

_____

_____

How it protects itself:

_____

_____

_____

Where it lives:

_____

_____

_____

Is it in danger of becoming extinct? Why?

_____

_____

_____

How it takes care of its young:

_____

_____

_____

Rain Forest Research Project *(cont.)*

Rain Forest Animals

Fill in the names of some animals from each layer of the rain forest.

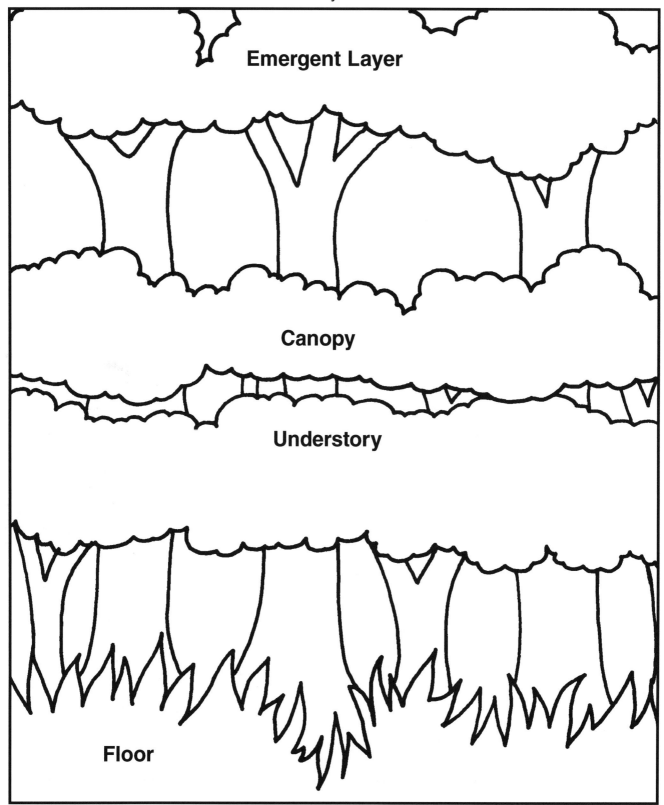

Emergent Layer

Canopy

Understory

Floor

Send a Message

Directions: Color and cut out the note card below. Fold the note so that the picture is on its front. Write to your congressperson and tell him or her why it is important to you to save the rain forest.

Create a Rain Forest Environment

Creating a rain forest environment provides a dramatic visual illusion that will capture your students' interest and imagination. (A sample classroom rain forest environment can be found on page 42.) The project has impact because it is so big. It is also a project your students will never forget! The goal is to gain awareness and appreciation for the beauty of the rain forest and to become educated about the danger of its demise and environmentally conscious about products, recycling, and saving our earth. This project will be a reminder of the story's moral, "What happens tomorrow depends on what you do today."

Before you begin constructing your classroom rain forest, distribute the following letter to students, local grocers, and merchants. (If necessary, acquire administrative approval prior to sending out letters.)

Dear_____,

We want to turn our classroom into a rain forest! Please help by collecting and donating any of the following items:

- Large sheets of cardboard
- Cardboard boxes
- Burlap in greens and browns
- Old sheets dyed green or brown
- Paper tubes (bathroom tissue or paper towel)
- Carpet rolls (for tree trunks)
- Wrapping paper
- Butcher paper
- Construction paper
- Styrofoam packing material
- String, rope, and cord
- Lots of newspaper
- Gallon milk jugs (for tree bases)
- Fishnet (for canopy)
- Tennis ball and frozen orange juice cans

- Glue gun and glue sticks
- Duct tape and masking tape
- Pipe cleaners
- Crepe paper streamers, brown and green
- Felt
- Tissue paper, large and small, all colors
- Watercolor, acrylic, and tempera paint
- Spray paint in brown, green, and gray
- Markers
- Christmas tree stands
- Raffia or Spanish moss
- Greenery (artificial, donated)
- Blue cellophane or plastic sheets
- Florist's wire

Thank you for the help!

_____
(signature)

Create a Rain Forest Environment *(cont.)*

Directions: Follow these step-by-step directions to create a beautiful rain forest environment in your classroom. For a concept of the finished classroom rain forest, see page 42. Invite some guests, including other students, parents, and administrators, to see this environment and use it to educate others about the rain forest.

1. **Walls and Windows**

   Cover the walls using fabric, burlap, wrapping paper, or butcher paper. Paint murals of green plants and leaves, flowers, trees, and vines on butcher paper. Paint some murals on the windows, leaving some space for light to filter through. Add some dish detergent to tempera paint.

   Cover one window with blue cellophane to simulate a waterfall. Surround it with "rocks" made from wadded-up newspaper held with masking tape and spray-painted realistically. (Ask parents and others if anyone has an electric fountain to donate.)

2. **Outside Perimeter of Classroom**

   Begin to build and place trees around the walls of the classroom. See Step #6 for instructions on how to make trees.

3. **Canopy**

   Suspend fishnet (which can be purchased inexpensively from party stores) about one foot to two feet (3m–6m) from the ceiling, leaving the middle of the room open. Weave raffia vines and leaves into the fishnet, or make vines by cutting long 6-foot (1.8 m) strips of brown butcher paper, crinkling it and then twisting it into vine shapes. Add brown and green crepe paper streamers for color.

4. **Kapok Tree**

   This is the centerpiece of your creation and should be placed in the middle of the room.

   Base: Place a carpet roll securely in a Christmas tree stand. Trunks can also be made by padding a 2" x 4" (5 cm x 10 cm) piece of wood with newspaper. For the wood tree, make a crossed wooden stand.

   Tree Trunk: Wrap the trunk in brown butcher paper, newspaper painted brown, or brown grocery bags. Secure this paper with a glue gun. Burlap or other fabric can also be used to wrap the trunk; secure it with the glue gun. Torn paper bags or other scraps can be glued to the trunk for texture.

   Branches: Gather real tree branches for your tree or make branches by rolling brown paper or fabric around yardsticks or wooden dowels. Secure these to the trunk with the glue gun. You may need to drill some holes in the trunk to hold the branches.

   Fringed leaves: Roll newspaper widthwise and tape the end. Make cuts at one end, cutting through all of the layers of the paper. Pull out the cut end carefully, and you will have fringed foliage. Experiment with different types of paper to make fringed foliage. More leaves are described in activity #6.

Create a Rain Forest Environment *(cont.)*

5. Floor

The floor should be covered with an assortment of Spanish moss, real leaves collected from the ground (not picked from living foliage), and cut scraps of paper. Bushes—smaller versions of trees described in activity #6—can be set in various places. Use donated greenery to fill in empty spaces.

6. Trees and Leaves

Trees: Make trees from paper tubes which can be slipped onto the legs of overturned desks, anchored on wooden crosses, or set into empty orange juice or tennis ball cans.

Leaves: Use the patterns on page 43 to draw, color, and cut out leaves.

7. Flowers

Tissue Paper Flowers: Use large and small pieces of tissue paper and florist's wire. To make two-color flowers, layer several large squares of tissue and then accordion-pleat them. Put the smaller pieces on top of the larger pieces and wire them together in the middle, leaving a length of the wire on one end. Tear the outer edges for a ragged effect, if desired. Then begin to pull and separate the paper and shape it into a large circle. These are easy to make and add color to your environment.

Construction Paper Flowers: Use the drawings on page 44 as a guide to make flowers from construction paper.

8. Animals

If time permits, make papier mâché animals such as a crocodile. Enlarge and color the animals on pages 24–26, 45 and 46 or use them as models for your own sketches. Then cut them out and glue them to cardboard boxes so that they will stand up. A monkey and a toucan are shown on page 12. You can also add small papier mâché or decorated paper snakes to your scene.

9. Anaconda Snake

Make a huge anaconda snake to wrap around the room. Use 20 feet to 25 feet (6 m to 7.5 m) of brown butcher paper. Crinkle it, then roll it, tapering one end for the tail. Make a head with an open mouth, eyes, and a long red tongue.

10. Butterflies and Insects

Using the patterns on pages 45 and 46 as a guide, make butterflies and other insects to inhabit your environment.

Create a Rain Forest Environment *(cont.)*

11. Birds

Make birds from construction paper or papier mâché, or create them using small boxes as forms. Hang them from the ceiling with string or place them in the trees. Use the patterns on page 45 as a guide. A toucan is shown on page 12.

12. Sounds

Play rain forest sounds in the background for effect. An audio-cassette tape entitled "Sounds of the Jungle and Tropical Rain Forest" can be obtained by contacting the Rain Forest Action Network on the Internet at http/www.ran.org/ran/. Similar tapes can also be found at bookstores and department stores.

13. Cookie Booth

Make and sell some cookies to raise money to save the rain forest (**Note:** Check school district policy first.) Donations can be sent to the World Wildlife Fund (see Bibliography, page 48).

Rain Forest Cookie Drops

Ingredients:

- $3/4$ cup shortening (180 mL)
- $1 1/4$ cup brown sugar (300 mL)
- 2 tablespoons milk (30 mL)
- 1 tablespoon vanilla (15 mL)
- 1 egg
- $1 3/4$ cups flour (400 mL)

- 1 teaspoon salt (5 mL)
- $3/4$ teaspoon baking soda (180 mL)
- $1/2$ cup chocolate chips (125 mL)
- $1/2$ cup shredded coconut (125 mL)
- $1/2$ cup nuts (125 mL)

Directions:

Heat oven to 375°F (190°C). Combine the first five ingredients and then add the remaining items. Drop teaspoonfuls of dough three inches (8 cm) apart on baking sheets.

Bake at 375°F (190°C) for 10 to 13 minutes.

14. Display

Invite some guests to experience your rain forest environment. Have students make their own invitations using a rain forest theme.

Create a Rain Forest Environment *(cont.)*

Sample of a Completed Classroom Rain Forest

Create a Rain Forest Environment *(cont.)*

Leaf Patterns

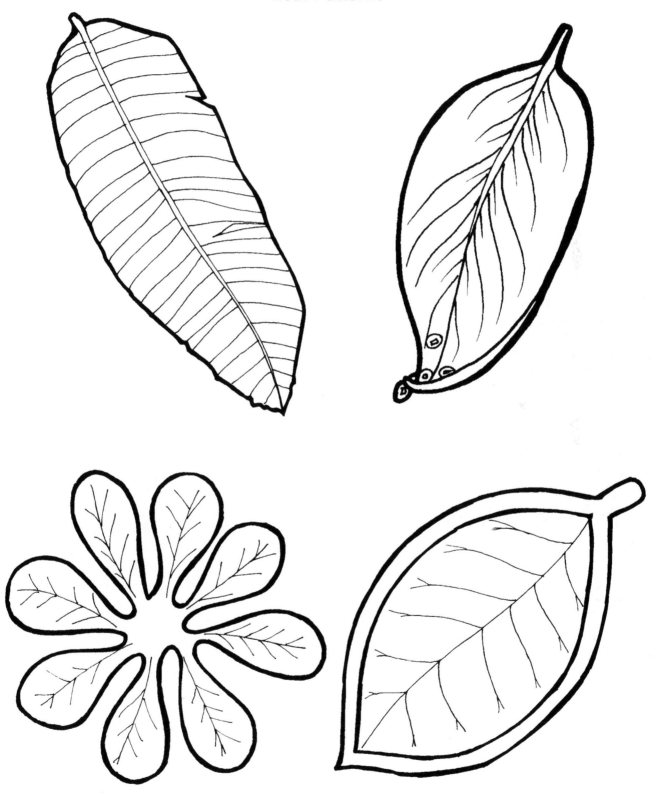

Create a Rain Forest Environment *(cont.)*

Flower Patterns

Create a Rain Forest Environment *(cont.)*

Animal Patterns

Create a Rain Forest Environment *(cont.)*

Animal Patterns *(cont.)*

Bibliography and Related Resources

Books About the Rain Forest

Baker, Jeannie. *Where the Forest Meets the Sea.* (Greenwillow, 1988)

Catterwell, Thelma. *Aldita and the Forest.* (Houghton Mifflin, 1989)

Cowcher, Helen. *Rain Forest.* (Farrar, Straus & Giroux, 1988)

Craig, Janet. *Wonders of the Rain Forest.* (Troll, 1990)

Forsyth, Andrian. *Journey Through a Tropical Jungle.* (Simon & Schuster, 1988)

Galdone, Paul. *The Monkey and the Crocodile.* (Ticknow and Fields, 1969)

George, Jean Craighead. *One Day in the Tropical Rain Forest.* (HarperCollins Child Books, 1990)

Goodman, B. *The Rain Forest.* (Little, Brown, 1991)

Hoff, Mary and Mary M. Rodgers. *Our Endangered Planet: Tropical Rain Forests.* (Lerner, 1991)

Johnson, Sylvia A. *Animals of the Tropical Forests.* (Lerner, 1976)

Norden, Carroll R., ed. *The Jungle.* (Steck Vaughn, 1988)

Podendorf, Illa. *Jungles.* (Children's Press, 1982)

Pratt, Kristin Joy. *A Walk in the Rain Forest.* (Dawn Publications, 1992)

Prelutsky, Jack. *Toucans Two and Other Poems.* (Macmillan, 1970)

Taylor, Barbara. *Rain Forest.* (Dorling Kindersley, Inc., 1992)

Van Allsburg, Chris. *Jumanji.* (Houghton Mifflin, 1981)

Wilkes, Angela. *Jungles.* (EDC, 1980)

Videotapes and Films

Cornet, Animals of the World Series: *Animals of South America.* Available from Cornet/MTI Film & Video, (800)777-8100. video

National Geographic Series. *STV: Rain Forest.* Available from Video Discovery, (800)548-3472. videodisc

National Wildlife Federation. *Our Threatened Heritage.* Available from International Program, 1412-16th St. NW, Washington, DC 20036. film

Patridge Film & Video. *Monkey Rain Forest.* Available from Cornet/MTI Film & Video, (800)777-8100. videodisc

World Wildlife Fund. *Vanishing Rain Forest Rap.* Available from P.O. Box 4866, Hampden Post Office, Baltimore, MD 21211, (202)293-4800). video

Software

Amazon Trail. MECC Software, published by Sunburst, P.O. Box 100, Pleasantville, New York 10570, (800)321-7511, http://www.nysunburst.com

Destination: Rain Forest. Imagination Express Series.

Eco Adventures in the Rain Forest. Chariot Software Group, 3659 India St., Suite 100C, San Diego, CA 92013-9722.

A Field Trip to the Rain Forest. Sunburst, (800)321-7511.

The Rain Forest, Volume 4. RE Media Software.

The Rain Forest: RE Media Software.

Scholastic's The Magic School Bus® Explores the Rainforest. Microsoft Corp., Redmond, CA (800)-426-9400.

Talking Jungle Safari. Orange Cherry Software. Available from CDL Software Shop, (800)637-0047.

Bibliography and Related Resources *(cont.)*

Organizations:

The Children's Rain Forest
P.O. Box 936
Lewiston, ME 04240
Write for material and a newsletter or to purchase rain forest acreage.

Conservation International
1015 18th St., NW
Suite 1000
Washington, DC 20036
"Rain Forest Teaching Kit" includes a study guide for a 25-minute video.

Cornell University Laboratory of Ornithology
159 Sapsucker Woods Rd.
Ithaca, NY 14850
A cassette of rain forest sounds is available.

EARTHWATCH
680 Mt. Auburn St.
Box 403
Watertown, MA 02272
A tropical rain forest curriculum is available.

Educational Images Ltd.
P.O. Box 3456, West Side
Elmira, NY 14905
"The Tropical Rain Forest Set" contains slides and a booklet.

National Wildlife Federation
1400 16th St., NW
Washington, DC 20036-2266
Nature Scope, Vol. 16, order #75044

Nature Recordings
P.O. Box 2749
Friday Harbor, WA 98250
A jungle sounds recording, "Jungle" can be ordered.

World Wildlife Fund and Conservation Foundation
1250 24th St., NW
Suite 500
Washington, DC 20037

25597631R00029

Printed in Poland
by Amazon Fulfillment
Poland Sp. z o.o., Wrocław